LIFE BEGINS AFTER COFFEE!

(A morning meditation.)

CONTENTS

PREFACE

All Things Coffee speaks to those who see coffee, not only as an enticing and exciting elixir, but also as a muse. An earthly gift from the divine unknown. A robust beverage. A versatile ingredient. A loyal friend in solitude. A persistent excuse to meet with a loved one. Poetry in a cup.

This book encompasses historical, cultural, health and social justice topics as well as fun facts and recipes, all revolving around coffee.

HISTORY

FABLE OF FIRST CUP OF COFFEE

It all starts with legends and folklore

Rather than facts that can be proven for sure.

But perhaps around 9th-century

Was when coffee first made history.

That's when a goatherder in Ethiopia

Discovered berries that gave his flock euphoria.

He told a monk about these magical beans,

But they were immediately forbidden it seems

As they were thrown into the fire

So that they would no longer inspire!

But out of the blaze came a perfume,

That made the nearby monks assume

What was burning would be good to consume.

Hence, they raked the roasted beans from the embers

And dissolved them in boiling water containers.

That's how the first coffee was served;

At least according to what one tale conveyed.

A BRIEF HISTORY OF COFFEE

Coffee beans were first cultivated in 15th century,

By Yemini Sufis who considered it a luxury.

They drank the dark beverage for spiritual intoxication

And stayed up all night to seek divine purification.

The sacred beverage spread like wildfire,

Throughout Middle East and Ottoman Empire.

By 16th century Europe got the news

Of the elixir that brews.

Soon coffee houses began to pop up,

To help all Europeans get perked up.

Then the Dutch took some coffee plants

And transferred them to East Indies and American lands.

The trees thrived in these continents,

Making coffee production one of their accomplishments.

Hence to this day most coffee comes

From these regions in bulks.

Of course by now coffee is prevalent;

And sought after with no equivalent.

6262 P. Z. - ALGER CAFÉ MAURE INTÉRIEUR

SOCIAL JUSTICE

THE BITTER TRUTH ABOUT FEMALE COFFEE WORKERS

Coffee is dark, bitter and complex. So is its politics. Today, 90 percent of coffee production takes place in developing countries, while the majority of coffee consumption is in industrialized countries. The average coffee worker gets a minimum wage of less than $3 a day. Ironically, this is how much the average American spends on coffee per day.

But getting an equivalent to sweatshop wage is not the sole issue for coffee farmers. They also have to work under repulsive conditions. Long and arduous hours of work, migrating from one field to another, sleeping in temporary shelters on bunk beds, as well as cooking, washing and bathing from the same water source are typical.

Globally, women make up over 70 percent of all the coffee farmers. In some countries, this percentage is even higher. For instance in Ethiopia, the sixth largest coffee producing country, nearly 80 percent of coffee farmers are women.

Aside from the day-to-day struggles coffee farmers face, these women must also juggle family life and deal with the machismo attitude that is prevalent throughout many developing countries. One can picture the typical female coffee worker as a scrawny woman with a baby tied on her back, going from one tree to another to pick coffee beans.

As coffee lovers, let us keep in mind that the cost of our daily java consumption may equal a female farmer's entire daily wage. But most importantly, let's do things that help the coffee community evolve toward a just and rewarding industry for all its workers, especially the women.

Here are some things we can do to help coffee farmers and growers:

• Buy fair trade coffee.

• Support coffee plantations that support their farmers.

• Advocate fair treatment of coffee farmers.

• Write and inform others about this issue.

HOW FAIR IS FAIR TRADE COFFEE?

If you're like most people in this country, chances are you drink coffee every day. And why shouldn't you? It tastes good, smells good, and lately, it's been getting a lot of good press. Published research and studies are claiming that drinking coffee may prevent or lower the risk of a wide variety of diseases such as: Parkinson's, Alzheimer's, heart disease, type 2 diabetes, liver and colon cancers, certain infections, as well as depression.

All this good news gets topped off by the fact that there are plenty of options when it comes to choosing your cup of joe: bold, mild, flavored, half caff, decaf, organic, etc. While personal taste is a key factor in making your choices, it may not be the only one. These days, many consumers also consider the social, ethical and environmental impacts of what they consume. For java drinkers, this consciousness is manifested through fair trade coffee. But what exactly is fair trade coffee and how fair is its claim?

First off, fair trade is not a brand; it's a qualifier or certification, like 'organic'. Fair trade coffee comes from many different regions around the world, but it has a certain set of criteria.

First and foremost, fair trade's goals are to ensure that the coffee workers are treated humanely and receive decent wages. In the world of coffee farming, this merely means that the farmers work in a safe environment, with reasonable working conditions, and at the end of a long, arduous day, they can feed their families. It also means they can send their children to school instead of having them work in the fields with them. (Fair trade strictly prohibits forced child labor, which is a common practice among coffee farmers.)

Secondly, fair trade aims to promote environmental sustainability. As such, all fair trade coffees need to be devoid of genetically modified organisms (GMOs) and harmful agrochemicals. Growers need to practice farming that maintains biodiversity and protects the land and wildlife. These include practices of water conservation, proper waste disposal, and so forth.

Thirdly, fair trade places an emphasis on providing farmers with business opportunities and skills needed to compete in the global marketplace. This includes arranging for independent interactions between the farmers and importers where the two parties do business as directly as possible in order to eliminate middlemen.

While there are other factors that go into making a fair trade coffee, these three are the prominent ones cited by advocates. So far, so fair, right?

FAIR · TRADE

FAIR TRADE . NOT FREE TRADE

Well, according to critics, fair trade is ambiguous and controversial. Several researches have pointed out shortcomings in this method of coffee producing. For example, few university studies, including those from the University of California (Berkeley, San Diego and San Francisco), Harvard, and the University of Wisconsin, point to the flaws of the fair trade system and question its effectiveness. Some argue that it doesn't address the root cause of poverty among coffee farmers. Critics also argue that the effects of this way of trading have been none to negligible, adding that fair trade has a long way to go to live up to its promises.

While there may be debates over the long-term benefits and effectiveness of fair trade, a couple of points need to be acknowledged. One is that fair trade does not make the already dire working situation of coffee growers any worse. At the very least it's neutral, whereas at best, it does make improvements, however slightly. Secondly, this system does have the intention to help coffee farmers by improving their living conditions and ending child labor. And while it takes a lot more than good intentions to achieve these goals, having good intentions is a great start. So if you're a coffee drinker and you choose fair trade, consider it a fair choice. A very fair choice!

HEALTH

DRINK TO YOUR LIVER

In the past decade or so, there have been numerous studies showing that coffee consumption may ward off several cancers, including: breast, colon, and liver.

In the case of the latter, coffee has particularly been potent in reducing the risk of hepatocellular carcinoma, a primary liver cancer that usually arises in patients with pre-existing cirrhosis.

Since one of the most common causes of cirrhosis is heavy alcohol use, it is safe to say coffee helps protect against the bad effects of booze. But to be clear, it's not safe to down as much alcohol as desired and merely rely on coffee to diminish its potential hazards. It's also important to note that although coffee reduces the risk of alcohol-related cirrhosis, it has no effect on cirrhosis caused by Hepatitis C.

Never the less, studies have consistently shown an inverse association between drinking coffee and primary liver cancer. In fact, the higher the coffee consumption, the lower the risk.

It's not clear what component in coffee causes this protection though. Since other caffeinated beverages like tea or Cola do not have the same effect, caffeine has been ruled out. Some researchers believe that the antioxidants (polyphenols or flavonoids) in coffee act as a buffer. But coffee has a complex chemistry, making it hard to pinpoint exactly what element may be responsible for this protection.

Never the less, the bottom line could be: if you've had too much to drink, it may be a good idea to pause and brew a cup, or even better, pot of coffee. Although the caffeine in coffee will not help you sober up (as some mistakenly believe), 'something' in coffee will act like a shield against the poisonous effects of too much alcohol. Now, cheers to that!

Fig. 3.

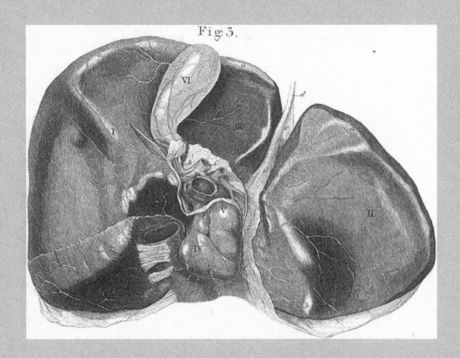

Fig. 4.

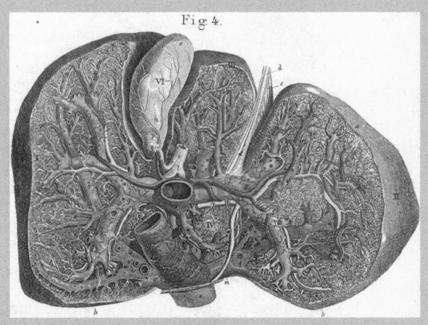

MORE COFFEE FOR HER COULD KEEP THE BLUES AT BAY

Many women believe that coffee is just a quick pick-me-up. Or at most, it helps them get through a hectic day. But when it comes to women's mental wellbeing and overall happiness, coffee does more than that.

A 2011 study led by Harvard School of Public Health found that women who drank four or more cups of coffee per day had 20% less chance of developing depression than those who drank little or none.*

Yet, it's not clear what in coffee contributes to the decrease in depression. Although caffeine is a brain stimulator, other caffeinated drinks such as tea, caffeinated soda, and hot chocolate do not provide the same results. Scientists suspect that the chemicals and antioxidants in coffee, rather than caffeine, may be natural mood enhancers.

While it's good to keep in mind that experts are not suggesting the more coffee a woman drinks, the happier and healthier she'll get, they are indicating that drinking four cups or more per day, decreases her chance of getting depressed.

But regardless of how many cups of coffee it takes to make a woman happy, she can rest assure that each tall, dark and hot cup of java is more than just a quickie!

*The study, "Coffee, Caffeine, and Risk of Depression Among Women," was published in the September 26, 2011, issue of the Archives of Internal Medicine.) https://www.hsph.harvard.edu/news/hsph-in-the-news/coffee-depression-women-ascherio-lucas/

FUN FACTS

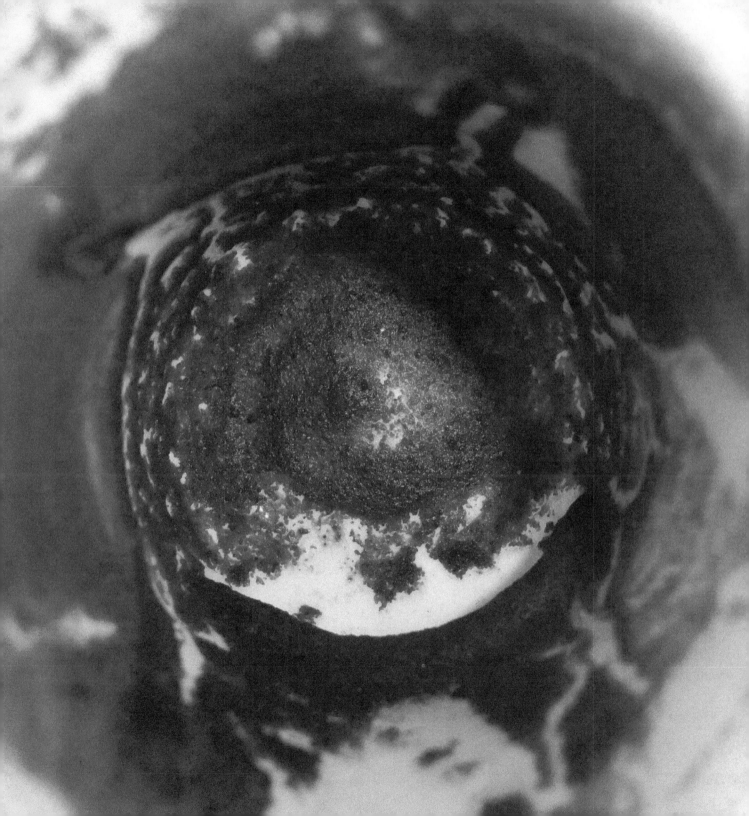

TASSEOGRAPHY

Coffee grounds are subject to interpretation. That is, if you're doing tasseography; a form of fortune telling where patterns of tea leaves or coffee grounds are interpreted based on the shapes and forms they make.

It is not clear when and where tasseography originated. Many believe the Gypsies started this practice. But then again, people in Asia and Middle East have interpreted the shapes of tea leaves and coffee prints from ancient times.

Perhaps some form of tasseography has always been around. Most likely, it started with our cavemen ancestors who aimed to make sense of the world around them by giving meaning to different shapes and forms. Certainly, the never-ending curiosity to find out what lies ahead influenced such readings. But more than curiosity, these readings may have been used to plan and prepare for the future.

But does tasseography reveal the truth and can it prepare us for what comes next? There are no proofs, however, that doesn't stop it from being a fun pastime. 'Reading cups', whether it's through tea leaves or coffee grounds, can be an interesting activity at a party or after a family dinner. It can stimulate conversations, bring people closer together and make gatherings more memorable.

If you ever plan to throw a tasseography party or simply want to do readings for friends, choosing to serve Turkish coffee could be a good thing. This kind of coffee has more residues and leaves more defined imprints than regular coffee or tea. Just make sure you follow the directions on its box since it's prepared differently than regular coffee or espresso.

To get started, here are some basic shapes and forms you can look for:

BIRDS: Good news

CAT: A deceitful friend or relative

EYE: Creation; you need more creativity in your life

FRUIT: Prosperity, result

LINES: If straight means progress, if wavy means uncertain path

OWL: Gossip, scandal

SCISSORS: Quarrel, even separation

WALL: An upcoming obstacle

THE MYSTERIOUS BLACK COFFEE

Question: What is Black Coffee; a dark beverage or a mystery play?
Answer: both.

Black Coffee, this universally known cup of java is also the name of Agatha Christie's very first stage play. Christie, a prominent crime and short stories writer who has been referred by the *Guinness Book of World Records* as the world's best-selling author of all time, wrote the play in 1929.

Black Coffee was not praised by Christie's agent who advised her not to pursue it on stage. Luckily, Christie did not listen to him and went about producing it. And not only the play turned out to be a long-lasting stage success, but it was later adapted into a novel as well as a movie.

The story is set in an English country house. Its owner, Sir Claud Amory, is a prominent scientist who has been working on a secret scientific formula which is potentially worth a fortune. Perhaps, when Christie famously said, "Coffee in England always tastes like a chemistry experiment," she was only referring to her play. But then again, England being a land of tea drinkers, her statement may have had a double meaning!

TO DRINK OR NOT TO DRINK

Most of us can't go a day without coffee. Long meetings, complicated work reports, major exams, and tiresome hours on the computer have one thing in common: coffee breaks. That's why it's a wonder that William Shakespeare, one of the most prominent and prolific playwrights of all time, who no doubt spent hours and hours writing and editing his plays, never sipped coffee. (Imagine writing Hamlet without it!)

But during Shakespeare's lifetime (1564 to 1616) coffee drinking was uncommon, if not unheard of. In fact, the first coffeehouse in England was not established until 1650s. Even tea, the most quintessential English beverage, was not publicly introduced till the 1660s. So there goes any possibility of a 'caffeine fix' for the famous author.

What did people drink during Shakespeare's time, you ask? Ale and wine were common as well as their diluted versions which were served even during breakfast. Yet, ale and wine incite the opposite effect of coffee and tea. They are calming and sedative which does not make them great choices for long work days. But they seemed to have worked fine for the hardworking English people at the time.

One wonders though, how coffee may have affected Shakespeare as a writer. Perhaps he would be an addict like many writers who faithfully depend on this beverage. One could easily imagine him spending long hours at a coffee shop, sipping double espressos, and writing his plays away.

In reality, however, it seems that Shakespeare needed no external boost to create his body of work. The stamina and creativity needed to compose his amazing comedies, tragedies, historical plays, and sonnets were fueled by something other than caffeine.

FRAPPÉ VERSUS FRAPPUCCINO

"When I grow up," said the little Frappe´, "I want to be a Frappuccino." Okay, so maybe this is not quite the way Frappe´ evolved into Frappuccino, but it doesn't sound unlikely either.

Frappuccino, simply put, is a fancy version of frappe´. Both beverages consist of powdered or instant coffee and ice. And both beverages are usually, but not always, sweetened with sugar or syrup. However, the origins of these two icy coffee drinks are quite different.

Frappe´ was an accidental invention of the Nestle´ company which occurred during The Thessaloniki International Trade Fair in 1957. Dimitris Vakondios, a representative of the company was exhibiting a chocolate beverage for children by mixing chocolate powder and cold milk in a shaker. During his break, he was looking for hot water to make his usual instant coffee, but could not find any. So he mixed the instant coffee with water and ice in the shaker and the very first Frappe´ was served.

Frappuccino, on the other hand, was originally invented by George Howell, the successful founder of the Boston-based company, The Coffee Connection. When Starbucks bought his company in 1994, Frappuccino became a registered trademark of Starbucks. Soon after, Frappuccino became a popular drink of this giant franchise.

While Frappe´ is popular in European countries, Frappuccino, with its usual additions of flavored syrup, whipped cream and chocolate topping is more popular in the U.S. No wonder Europeans think Americans have a love affair with sugar!

POEMS

SHAKESPEARE-INSPIRED SONNET

Shall I compare thee to an excellent cup of coffee?

Though you are sweeter than an extra sweetened mocha,

And bolder than a cup of Kenya,

More vibrant than espresso is your devotion,

And richer than Colombian coffee are your emotions;

It is no wonder your presence is addictive,

And so how lucky that you are also attentive;

You're the perfect blend of goodness,

With a hint of a mysterious smoothness;

So, shall I compare thee to an excellent cup of coffee?

If a comparison is to be shallow and carefree;

But then let me just add this:

So long as coffee is black and stimulating,

So long will your love be invigorating.

AN ODE TO THE STUDY COMPANION

It's that time of the year again,

When school days begin.

Mornings start and end in classes,

And nights are seen through reading glasses.

Homework, tests and finals,

Affect all the vitals.

Hours, minutes and seconds,

Are spent studying solo or with friends.

It's now that we realize,

One companion should be idolized.

Of all the great study buddies,

No one lasts this long during the studies.

Patient, strong and consistent,

Yet, a calm and inconspicuous coexistent.

Always there to warm us up,

Cheer us up or wake us up.

The one and only coffee,

Bitter as citrus rind or sweet as toffee.

HUMOR

TWELVE SIGNS YOU MAY BE A COFFEEHOLIC

Do you ever wonder if you're addicted to coffee? If this question has ever crossed your mind, then there's a good chance that you may be a coffeeholic, or at risk of becoming one. No need to panic though! Although addiction could be a serious problem, it's not always a bad thing. In fact, some addictions are 'good', or at the very least, okay. For example, addiction to working out, cooking, or reading novels could reduce stress and have long-term benefits.

Since numerous research and studies have revealed that drinking coffee may prevent or lower the risk of a wide variety of diseases such as: Type 2 diabetes, heart disease, certain cancers and infections, as well as depression, coffee addiction can also fall in the 'good' category.

Now that fear is out of the equation, read the following signs and symptoms to find out if you are a coffeeholic in the first place. (Just bear in mind that these are not based on medical or scientific evidence!)

1 Coffee is the first thing on your mind when you wake up in the morning. You may think this is quite common or 'normal'. You may be right. However, if coffee is one of the main reasons you get out of bed, then it may be a sign. If it's the ONLY reason, then it's definitely a sign.

2 You're like a coffee encyclopedia. You know a lot about coffee, whether it's nutritional, medical or historical facts. When among friends, you share coffee-related quotes and fun facts. You can even recite poetry in this genre.

3 You like to serve coffee to your guests. In fact, you insist on serving them coffee even when they say they prefer tea.

4 You just don't get tea drinkers. You don't have any fond memories from tea parties, worst yet, you associate the term with a political group you're not a fan of.

5 You plan your vacations around coffee. You do a 'Top Ten Coffee Hot Spots in the World' search, and go from there. Your next trip- fingers crossed-will be to Sumatra.

6 You also plan your social activities around coffee. When meeting with friends, you bypass the bar and restaurant scenes and meet them at a local coffee shop.

7 Everyone brings you coffee as souvenir. Whether your friends and loved ones travel near or far, east or west, to exotic or ordinary places, they always bring you the same thing: A bag of coffee.

8 You've considered a career in coffee. You may be a CPA, administrator, engineer, graphic designer, etc. Still, when it comes to choosing an industry to work for, coffee tops the list. Plus, your career role model is Howard Shultz.

9 Instead of a memoir, you're writing a book about coffee. This is despite the fact that you've had a very interesting life (i.e. you survived a nuclear war, your childhood friend was an ostrich, and you spent three years circumnavigating the world on a pool float that was shaped like a giant doughnut).

10 Your furniture and closet consist mostly of brown hues. In particular mocha, coffee and carob colors.

11 You can smell coffee from every corner of your house, not only the kitchen. That is because there are coffee-scented candles everywhere. Plus, your bathroom's air freshener is called 'Coffee Heaven' and your body wash is Sephora's 'Coffee and Cream'.

12 You proudly admit that you are a coffeeholic. You feel zero shame or guilt and need not to refer to any silly signs and symptoms chart.

DRINKS AND DESSERTS

TOPSY-TURVY ICED LATTE

The culinary world has plenty of room for bending the rules. You can have dessert for breakfast, breakfast for dinner, or make a main dish out of snacks. In fact, if there's one domain where it's safe and fun to play with the rules, it's the culinary world.

Topsy-turvy iced latte is one of those rule-breaking recipes where coffee ice cubes replace the usual coffee. As the cubes melt, coffee diffuses into the milk, slowly turning it into a rich iced latte.

The recipe also makes for a visually stimulating beverage.

INGREDIENTS:

- Brewed coffee (strong coffee is recommended)
- Cold milk of your choice (cow, soy, coconut, almond, etc.)

DIRECTIONS:

- Brew strong coffee and let it cool completely at room temperature.
- Pour the cooled coffee into ice cube trays and freeze.
- Fill a tall glass with generous amount of coffee ice cubes.
- Pour your favorite milk over it.

SUGARLESS COCO CRÈME MACCHIATO

"A spoonful of sugar helps the medicine go down." And it helps coffee too. Hence, exists a huge market of sugary coffee creamers, syrups, toppings, etc. But as science claims, sugar comes with health consequences.

So instead of focusing on the added sugar that comes with many popular and fancy coffee drinks such as, mocha, caramel macchiato or vanilla latte, lets put the spotlight on a recipe that embraces the main ingredients of such drinks, minus the sugar.

Coco crème macchiato is an espresso drink that looks like a mocha, but tastes more like a cappuccino. In other words, it's not sweet and contains no added sugar.

Just like cappuccino, the main ingredients are espresso and milk. The difference, however, is the topping which is a fancy dollop chocolaty whipped cream. How is that possible without sugar, you ask? Here's how: after you make your macchiato, you beat the heavy cream till it becomes whipped cream, but instead of adding sugar to it, you add unsweetened cocoa. And that's all there's to it. You now have a fancy café drink where a good amount of fat (from heavy cream) and antioxidant (from cocoa) has replaced the nutritionally cheap sugar.

INGREDIENTS:

- 2 shots of espresso
- ⅓ cup steamed milk of your choice
- ⅓ cup heavy whipping cream
- Unsweetened cocoa to taste

DIRECTIONS:

- In a bowl, whisk the heavy whipping cream and unsweetened cocoa with a whisker or an electric mixer till thickened.
- Prepare your macchiato using an espresso machine.
- Top your drink with a generous amount of chocolaty whipped cream.

BREAKFAST COFFEE ON THE GO

In some European countries, such as Italy and France, a latte or cappuccino may make a complete breakfast. In the U.S., however, such beverages are often considered part of the breakfast.

But these beverages could easily be a complete breakfast. After all, they contain milk which has fat, protein, calcium, minerals and vitamins. If this is not convincing enough to those who are breakfast-conscious, adding a scoop of protein powder should do the trick.

For a truly delicious and nutritious breakfast, try the following recipe. It can be made hot or cold and will have the nutritional benefits of a protein shake, as well as the caffeine fix of coffee. A great way to start the day in any country!

INGREDIENTS:

- 3 shots of espresso or ½ cup of strong coffee

- 1 cup milk of your choice (cow, soy, coconut, almond, etc.)

- 1 heaping scoop vanilla-flavored protein powder (whey or vegan)

DIRECTIONS:

- Make the espresso, or, if you don't have an espresso machine, brew strong coffee.

- Heat the milk if you'd like to serve the drink hot. Otherwise, skip this step.

- Blend all the ingredients in a blender. Serve in a tall glass (if cold) or mug (if hot).

WHEN COFFEE MEETS CHOCOLATE

Some pairs, like Romeo and Juliet or Dante and Beatrice, are romantic. Some pairs, like eyes or ears, are biological. Some, like action and reaction, are part of the laws of physics. But some pairs, like coffee and chocolate, are just delicious!

Of course, chocolate could pair well with many things. For example, wine and fruit go well with chocolate. Yet, there's something divine about pairing any shade of chocolate with coffee. Perhaps it's because the sweetness of chocolate enhances the bitterness of coffee (and vice versa).

For the ultimate coffee and chocolate combination, try the following Coffee Meets Chocolate dessert, and you might be convinced that some pairs are just meant to be!

INGREDIENTS:

- 1 pint heavy whipping cream
- 12 oz white chocolate chips
- 3 tbsp instant coffee
- 2 envelopes (¼ ounce each) unflavored gelatin
- ⅓ cup cold water

DIRECTIONS:

- Mix gelatin with cold water and let stand for few minutes.
- Mix heavy whipping cream with chocolate chips and cook on low till chocolate is melted.
- Add gelatin to whipping cream and chocolate mixture and mix till everything is completely dissolved. Remove from heat and let the mixture cool completely.
- Pour mixture in a pan and refrigerate for two hours or till firm.

FOR THE SHAKE OF COFFEE

Coffee shakes are great! Not only they provide caffeine, the energy-boosting companion of the everyday working person, but they're also reminiscent of much simpler times: childhood. A time when rich and sugary desserts did not equal calories and cholesterol, but simply, heavenly delights. For these reasons, a coffee shake makes the perfect 'adult treat'.

Many beverages are mistaken for coffee shakes. Frappes and Frappuccinos are two examples. But in fact, such drinks are often different versions of iced coffee; a combination of coffee, milk or powdered milk and syrup. Real coffee shakes should have two main ingredients: ice cream and coffee. Milk, cream and chocolate syrup may also be added.

Recipes vary, but if they're too fancy and include some kind of mixed powder, chances are, they're not shakes. After all, a shake is not a shake without ice cream!

So for the shake of coffee, make it simple and use the real deal ingredients. The following is a simple recipe:

INGREDIENTS:

- 1 cup vanilla ice cream
- ¼ cup chilled strong coffee
- Whipped cream and chocolate syrup for garnish (optional)

DIRECTIONS:

- Make some robust coffee and let it chill in the fridge for at least an hour.
- Blend the coffee and ice cream in a blender and pour into a tall shake glass.
- Garnish with whipped cream and chocolate syrup, if desired.

CARIBOU MARTINI

You would never think that coffee and champagne would go well together, but they do. Caribou martini proves this point. Made part with champagne and part with coffee flavored vodka, this martini is a unique blend of fruity flavors of champagne and bitter taste of coffee.

Caribou makes an excellent brunch cocktail. After all, just like its famous brunch counterpart, Mimosa, it's mostly champagne.

For best results, chill everything beforehand. That includes the champagne, vodka and the martini glasses.

INGREDIENTS:

- Chilled champagne
- Chilled coffee flavored vodka
- Berries for garnish (optional)

DIRECTIONS:

- In a chilled martini glass pour coffee flavored vodka till it's ¼ full.
- Fill the rest of the glass with champagne.
- Garnish with berries (optional).

CHOCOLATE WHITE RUSSIAN

You heard it right! C.H.O.C.O.L.A.T.E White Russian; a chocolaty and not-too-familiar version of the White Russian.

Like its original rival, this cocktail mainly consists of vodka and coffee liqueur. The difference is the added chocolate ingredient. Depending on which recipe you follow, the source of chocolate could be chocolate syrup, chocolate shavings, or simply cocoa powder poured on top.

Unlike what its name implies, White Russian was not originated in Russia but named in honor of its main ingredient, vodka. Although there are speculations as to where and when the drink originated, it's likely that it was first served in the late 1940s in the United States as Black Russian.

But if the origin of White Russian is ambiguous, the origin of Chocolate White Russian is even more ambiguous. Most likely, someone thought chocolate would be a harmonious addition to vodka and coffee liqueur. (S/he was right!)

Served over ice, Chocolate White Russian makes an excellent after dinner drink.

INGREDIENTS:

- 1 shot vodka
- 1 shot coffee liqueur
- 2 shots half and half
- Ice
- Chocolate shavings for decoration

DIRECTIONS:

- Pour vodka and coffee liqueur into a glass full of ice. Float half and half on top and stir. Top with chocolate shavings.

COFFEE-RIMMED TAMARIND MARGARITA

Tarter and darker than a classic margarita, this cocktail has an earthy look and taste to it. If you've never tried tamarind, be ready for a sour surprise.

First and foremost, get a hold of good quality tamarind puree. Most ethnic supermarkets and specialty food shops carry it. To get the most authentic taste, choose a product that is purely tamarind, or at least, doesn't have a lot of additives.

The rest of ingredients are standard for margarita (tequila, syrup and lime juice). When you have all the ingredients, combine in a blender and blend.

Salt or no salt? Neither. You'll need something that matches the earthiness of the cocktail, like coffee.

Either ground or instant coffee will do. Pour some of the coffee into a plate, then, wet the outside rim of the margarita glass with fresh lime and dab it into coffee. Slowly turn the rim till the entire outer edge is covered with coffee. *Now* your tamarind margarita is ready to be sipped. Salute!

INGREDIENTS:

- ⅓ cup tamarind puree
- ½ shot fresh lime juice
- 2 shots tequila
- ½ shot simple or maple syrup
- Few ice cubes
- Ground or instant coffee (for garnish)

DIRECTIONS:

- Combine all the ingredients in a blender and blend till frothy. Pour into a coffee-rimmed glass.

NEW YEAR'S EVE COCKTAIL LIST

Sipping cocktails on New Year's Eve can greatly enhance that "out with the old, in with the new" celebratory mood. Plus, what better way to welcome the new year than with a big, boozy cheer.

But too many cocktails can make one lethargic and sleepy. Don't' let this happen to you! Especially not on New Year's Eve. So what to do? Not to worry, you can have your cocktails and stay up too. Drinking cocktails with coffee is a great way to add some caffeine to boost your energy.

Fortunately, there are plenty of coffee-based cocktail recipes out there. And even more fortunately, they are rather easy to make. In fact, there's a standard way of making most coffee cocktails. Here's how:

• Start with an elegant cocktail glass. Bear in mind, you drink with your eyes first, so the more elegant and beautiful the glass, the more enhanced the experience.

• Pour a shot (or two, or three, or…you get the point) of your favorite liquor into the glass.

• Fill up half of the glass with either fresh-brewed coffee or iced coffee. If you prefer the latter, it's best to brew fresh coffee and let it chill in the fridge for about an hour. You can also add espresso instead of coffee. If you go the espresso route, make sure you add at least two shots to get enough liquid in your beverage.

• Top off the glass with some kind of dairy. Good choices are: half and half, heavy cream, condensed milk, sweetened creamer, and/or whipped cream. You can stick to one kind of dairy, or mix a few.

• Garnish is always optional, but highly recommended. (Don't forget that New Year's Eve is the perfect time to be flamboyant.)

Now that you know how to make a standard coffee cocktail, go ahead and create your own. And in case you need some help getting started, here's a list of some of the most well-known coffee cocktails.

AMERICAN COFFEE with Bourbon

AUSTRALIAN COFFEE with Bundaberg Rum

BRANDY COFFEE with Brandy

CARAJILLO with Anís

CORFU COFFEE with Koum Quat

ENGLISH COFFEE with Gin

FRENCH COFFEE with Grand Marnier

FRIAR'S COFFEE with Frangelico

GAELIC COFFEE with Whisky

GERMAN COFFEE with Schnapps

ITALIAN CLASSICO with Amaretto

JAMAICAN COFFEE with Rum

KAFFEKASK with Schnapps

KÚMEN KAFFI with Brennivín

MONK'S COFFEE with Bénédictine

PARISIENNE COFFEE or **CAFE ROYALE** with Cognac or Armagnac

RUSSIAN COFFEE with Vodka

SEVILLE COFFEE with Cointreau

SHIN SHIN COFFEE with Rum

SKYE COFFEE with Drambuie

THE REAL FOUL ONE with Absinthe

WHISKY COFFEE with Whisky

WITCH'S COFFEE with Strega

ACKNOWLEGMENTS

I often joke that if it wasn't for coffee, I wouldn't have made it all these years. But in reality, if it wasn't for the love and support of my family and friends, I truly wouldn't have made it all these years!

There are too many lovely people to name here; so, I spare the readers from a long list of names by saying that I hope that those who have a place in my heart know who they are, if or when, they read this!

Also, thanks to the people who helped me with this book: Geoff Borin for his amazing design; Julia Richardson for her thoughtful editorial guidance; and the photographers/illustrators:

Gabriel Garcia Marengo, front cover
Ping News, p.2
Nick Vandenberg, p. 5
Medin Pitarevic, p. 8
Ashley Van Haeften, p. 11
DFID - UK Department for International Development, p.14
Wavebreak Media, p.17
Qasim Zafar, p.21
Artem Beliaikin, p.22
Heather McQuaid, p. 26
Ninian Reid, p.29
Pedro Ribeiro Simões, p.30
Ada Be, p.33

Norma Dorothy, p.37
Marco Verch, p.38
Tarnay Nataliya, p.43
Nathan Dumlao p.47
Daisuke1230, p.48
Lemon 168, P.51
David Greenwood, p.52
Jonathan Borba, p.55
Louise Lyshoj, p.56
Jeppe Monster, p.59
Suri Pistols, p.60
Everett Collection, p.63
Michael Stout, p.64
Jack Randall, author photo p.66
Marco Verch, back cover

ABOUT THE AUTHOR

Ever since trying her first cup of coffee, purchased from her college campus's vending machine, Farnaz Calafi fell in love with this "magical beverage". With java as her favorite study companion, she studied Environmental Analysis and Design at the University of California, Irvine and went on to get her Master's degree in Journalism from Syracuse University. After graduation, she worked for the *Los Angeles Times* for several years before moving to New York, New York where she wrote for *Examiner.com* as the 'Manhattan Coffee Examiner'. She's currently transplanted back to California, and although a New Yorker at heart, she's grateful for the abundance of sunny days and beautiful beaches in the golden state. She is a fan and advocate of fact-based, well-researched journalism as well as thought-provoking opinion pieces that make the readers spit out their coffee! Her OpEd pieces have been published in *USA Today* and *The New York Times*.

Photograph by Jack Randall

ISBN 978-0-578-76271-5

CPSIA information can be obtained
at www.ICGtesting.com
Printed in the USA
BVHW010538211120
593641BV00003B/30